British Association for the Advancement of Science

On the North-Western Tribes of Canada

British Association for the Advancement of Science

On the North-Western Tribes of Canada

ISBN/EAN: 9783337878559

Printed in Europe, USA, Canada, Australia, Japan

Cover: Foto ©Andreas Hilbeck / pixelio.de

More available books at **www.hansebooks.com**

Fourth Report of the Committee, consisting of Dr. E. B. TYLOR, Dr. G. M. DAWSON, General Sir J. H. LEFROY, Dr. DANIEL WILSON, Mr. R. G. HALIBURTON, *and* Mr. GEORGE W. BLOXAM (*Secretary*), *appointed for the purpose of investigating and publishing reports on the physical characters, languages, and industrial and social condition of the North-Western Tribes of the Dominion of Canada.*

THE Committee report that, in addition to Mr. Wilson, of Sault Ste. Marie, who contributes some valuable remarks upon the Sarcee Indians, they have been enabled to secure the services of Dr. Franz Boas (now of New York, and one of the editors of 'Science'), who has been for several years engaged in ethnological investigations in America, particularly among the Eskimo and in British Columbia, and who has consented to return to that province for the purpose of continuing his researches there on behalf of the Committee, and in accordance with the instructions comprised in their 'Circular of Inquiry.' Only eight or nine weeks—in May, June, and July last were available for his trip, but, with the advantage of the experience and information obtained in his previous journey, he has been able to gather a large mass of valuable material. The results of his inquiries will be given in his final report, to be presented next year. For the present occasion he has prepared some preliminary notes, with an introductory letter (addressed to Mr. Hale), containing a brief account of his proceedings, and some important suggestions concerning future inquiries and the condition of the Indians of that province. The letter is as follows :—

'I beg to transmit the following report of my proceedings, with preliminary notes on the results of my researches in British Columbia. In your instructions dated May 22, 1888, you made it my particular object, on the present trip, to obtain as complete an account as possible of the coast tribes and their languages. As on my previous journey, in the winter of 1886-87, I had collected a considerable amount of material respecting the southern tribes, I turned my attention at once to the Indians inhabiting the northern parts of the coast, including the Tlingit. On June 1 I arrived in Vancouver, and after ascertaining certain doubtful points regarding the Skqomish, who live opposite the city, I proceeded to Victoria on June 3. Mayor J. Grant, of that city, kindly gave me permission to take anthropometric measurements of such Indians as were in gaol. This proved the more valuable, as the natives were very reluctant to have any measurements taken. I sought to obtain measurements and drawings of skulls in private collections in Victoria, and was fortunate enough to be able to measure eighty-eight skulls from various parts of the coast. The results of these measurements must be reserved for the final report. I will mention only the remarkable fact that skulls of closely related tribes show great and constant differences. Comparisons of ten skulls each from Victoria, Saanitch, and Comox give the following results :—

	Length Mill	Length-breadth Index	Length height Index
Victoria	184·5	77·7	75·0
Sanitch	161·0	95·5	80·8
Comox	176·6	79·9-	77·1

These differences are in part due to artificial deformation. It seems, however, that this explanation is not sufficient. These tribes belong to the Salish stock.

'As soon as an opportunity offered to start northward, I left Victoria and stayed the greater part of June in Port Essington, where I studied the customs and language of the Tsimshian, and obtained notes on the Haida. When returning to Victoria a few Heiltsuk from Bella Bella were on board the vessel, and I obtained notes on this tribe, which supplement to some extent my former observations. After my return to Victoria I took up the Tlingit and Haida languages, and when several canoes from the west coast of Vancouver Island arrived, that of the Nutka. In the beginning of July, Father J. Nicolai, who is thoroughly conversant with the Nutka language, arrived there from Kayokwaht, and in a number of conversations gave me valuable information regarding the grammar of that language. I obtained information respecting their legends and customs from a few natives, and on July 11 went to the mainland. After staying two days in Lytton I proceeded to Golden and up the Columbia river, in order to devote the rest of the available time to the Kootenay. On July 26 I returned east.

'The results of my reconnoissance are necessarily fragmentary, as I was not able to devote more than a few days to each tribe. I obtained, however, sufficient material to determine the number of linguistic stocks, and the number of important dialects of those stocks which I visited. The vocabularies which I collected during my former and on the present trip contain from 500 to 1,000 words, and embrace the following languages: Tlingit, Haida, Tsimshian, Kwäkiutl (Heiltsuk and Lekwiltok dialects), Nutka, Salish (Bilqula, Pentlatsh, Comox, Nanaimo, Lkungen, Sishiatl, Skqomish, Ntlakápamuq dialects), and Kootenay. I obtained, also, grammatical notes on all these languages, and texts in some of them.

'I may be allowed to add a few remarks on future researches on the ethnology of British Columbia. Only among the tribes from Bentinck Arm to Johnson Strait the customs of the natives may be studied uninfluenced by the whites. But here, also, their extinction is only a question of a few years. Catholic missionaries are working successfully among the Nutka; the fishing and lumbering industries bring the natives of the whole coast into closer contact with the whites. In all other parts of the country, except on the upper Skeena, the student is, to a great extent, compelled to collect reports from old people who have witnessed the customs of their fathers, who heard the old myths told over and over again. In the interior of the province even these are few, and it is only with great difficulty that individuals well versed in the history of olden times can be met with. After ten years it will be impossible in this region to obtain any reliable information regarding the customs of the natives in pre-Christian times. Even the languages are decaying since the advent of the whites and on account of the extensive use of Chinook. Young people neither understand the elaborate speeches of old chiefs nor the old songs and legends when properly told. Even the elaborate grammatical rules of these languages are being forgotten. For instance, old Nutka will never form the plural of the verb without reduplication, while young men almost always omit it. Instead of the numerous modi, phrases are used—in short, the languages are decaying rapidly. The study of the anthropological features of these races is also becoming more and more difficult on account of their frequent intermarriages with whites; and the consequent difficulty of finding full-blood Indians. The once abundant material of old native crania and skeletons lying scattered all over the province is becoming more and more scarce as it decays and the country is being reclaimed.

' It is nowhere sufficient to study languages alone in order to solve ethnological problems; but in this province the study of a large amount of anthropological material is an absolute necessity on account of the diversity of languages and the great dialectic differences in some of them. The Salish stock in British Columbia, for instance, is spoken in eleven dialects, which are each unintelligible to the speakers of the others. It would be of great importance to study the anthropological features of this race, the northern tribes of which are physically very much like the Kwäkintl.

' Last of all I mention the antiquities of the province. Valuable relics are destroyed every day. They are turned up by the plough and thrown away: graves and mounds are levelled, shell heaps are used for manuring purposes, cairns are removed. The destruction will be very thorough, as those parts in which relics are found are at the same time those which are the earliest to be reclaimed.

' For all these reasons an early study of the ethnology of the province must be considered a necessity. In the course of a few years much might be done to preserve the most important facts. The languages might be reduced to writing, the interesting poems and songs that are still afloat might be preserved, we might obtain a complete account of the mythology, and sufficient material for anthropological researches. A few years hence it will be impossible to obtain a great part of the information that may now be gathered at a comparatively slight expense.

' I cannot close these remarks without adding a few words on the present state of the Coast Indians. It is well known that they have been greatly reduced in numbers since the advent of the whites, and that they are still diminishing. It is also well known that, with few exceptions, they have made no progress whatever. The reasons for these facts are easily understood; the natives become accustomed to products of our manufacture, and in order to purchase them become servants while they have been masters before. At the same time their native industries decay. This process is hastened by the influence of missionaries, who discourage all native arts, as connected with their heathenish customs, without being able to supply anything in their stead. Thus the psychical life of the natives is impoverished, and this, I think, accounts principally for their rapid degradation after the first contact with the whites. The only way to civilise these tribes is clearly shown by Mr. W. Duncan's success at Metlakahtla. He made the Indians of Metlakahtla a self-sustaining, independent community. Similar results are gradually being obtained in other places, and these results show that the establishment of independent industries on co-operative principles will educate the Indians and make them capable of becoming useful members of the State. The easiest and soundest way to do this is to encourage native industries and arts—fishing and working in wood. At the same time the natives ought to be educated to a more sanitary way of living. This can be attained only by putting energetic medical men in charge of Indian districts. There can be no doubt that an intelligent man, capable of adjusting his argument to the mind of the Indian, would easily induce them to a thorough sanitation. The Indians do not individually give up their old customs, but invariably do so in council. By gaining their confidence, the council could be easily induced to listen to sound advice. I do not believe that it is too late to save the Indian from utter destruction; and we may still hope that the spectacle of an intelligent race becoming more and more degraded and vanishing from the earth's surface will cease to exert its saddening influence upon the traveller who visits the shores of British Columbia.'

To this letter Dr. Boas adds the following :—

PRELIMINARY NOTES ON THE INDIANS OF BRITISH COLUMBIA.

Although the Indians of the north-west coast of America belong to a great number of linguistic stocks, and although their physical peculiarities suggest that they belong to various races, their customs are so much alike that it is impossible to describe one tribe without having reference to all the others. For this reason it is necessary in a general survey to treat their languages and their physical and ethnographical character separately, although from the standpoint of the psychologist it would seem more desirable to describe each tribe by itself.

The following are the principal races inhabiting the province, including the coast strip of Alaska: 1. the Tinnè (or Tinneh), who occupy the interior from the extreme north to Quesnelle and Chilcot in the south. 2. The Tlingit, on the coast of Alaska; and the Haida, on Queen Charlotte Islands and the southern part of Prince of Wales Archipelago. 3. The Tsimshian, on Nass and Skeena Rivers and the adjoining islands. 4. The Kwākiutl, from Douglas Channel to the central part of Vancouver Island, excepting the west coast of that island and Dean Inlet and Bentinck Arm. 5. The Nutka, of the west coast of Vancouver Island and Cape Flattery. 6. The Salish, on the south-eastern part of Vancouver Island, on the mainland as far as Quesnelle Lake and Selkirk Range, and on Bentinck Arm. 7. The Kutonaqa, on Kootenay Lake and River, and on the Upper Columbia.

[Dr. Boas here gives brief notes on the grammatical structure peculiar to each of the six linguistic stocks which he has studied—the Tlingit (and Haida), Tsimpshian, Kwākiutl, Nutka, Salish, and Kutonaqa. It has seemed advisable, however, to defer the publication of these notes until they can appear in fuller form in the final report, where they will be accompanied by the comparative vocabularies and the ethnographical map, and can have the benefit of the author's revision of the proofs.

In the Indian words comprised in this report the vowels are to be pronounced as in Italian, and the consonants, for the most part, as in English. The letters k‛ and g‛ represent deep gutturals corresponding to the ordinary k g. The h represents the German ch in ich. The q denotes the sound of the Scotch ch in loch. By ll an exploded l is indicated, and by k‛ an exploded ku, the u pronounced very indistinctly.]

SOCIAL ORGANISATION.

I confine myself, in these preliminary notes, to a brief description of the totemism of these tribes, leaving a more detailed discussion of the prerogatives of the chiefs and of certain families to the final report. Among the Tlingit and Haida we find a great number of crests, which, however, are divided into two groups—the raven and the wolf among the Tlingit, the raven and the eagle among the Haida. The Tsimshian have four totems, the raven (called K·anhu'da), the eagle (Laqski'yek), the wolf (Laqkyebö'), and the bear (Gyīspōtue'dā). The Hēiltsuk and their northern neighbours have three totems; the killer (*Delphinus orca*) (Ha'uq'ai/ᵗtēnoq), the raven (K·ö'i/ᵗtēnoq), and the eagle (Wik'oaq/ᵗtēnoq). It is a very remarkable fact that among the other tribes of Kāwkiutl lineage no totemism, in its strict meaning, is found. The tribes enumerated above have the system of relationship in the female line. The child belongs to the mother's crest, and, although the wife follows her husband to his village, the children, when grown up, always return to their mother's tribe. I conclude from the fact that the Kwākiutl, south of Rivers Inlet, have the system of relationship in the male line, or, more properly speaking, in both lines; that the Hēiltsuk adopted their system of totems from the Tsimshian. I have not heard a single tradition to the effect that the gentes consider themselves the descendants of their totem ; the Tlingit and Haida, as well as the Tsimshian and Hēiltsuk, have certain traditions referring to ancestors who had encounters with certain spirits or animals who gave them their crests. It is true that the Haida and Tlingit claim to have been created by the raven, but the legend has no reference whatever to the totem. The Kwākiutl and Salish tribes are also divided into gentes, but these are not distinguished by animal totems, but derive their origin each from a man who was sent down from heaven by the deity, and who, in some way or other, obtained his crest from a spirit. These legends are of the same character as the corresponding ones of the Tsimshian. The crest of the family is represented on paintings on the house fronts, on the 'totem posts,' and on tattooings. The latter are probably not used by the Tlingit, while the Haida tattoo breast, back, arms, and legs. The Tsimshian tattoo only the wrists, according to their crest. Tattoo marks are also used by the Nutka. The figures on posts and houses have always a reference to the being encountered by the ancestor, but sometimes also figures of the father's crest are used by the owner, the father having the right to permit his child to use them. The posts do not represent a continuous story, but every figure refers to one tradition. Each gens has also names of its own, which among the Tsimshian must have a reference to the father's gens. Thus, on hearing a name a Tsimshian knows at once to what gens both the bearer and his father belong. Among the Salish and Kwākiutl the child follows, as a rule, the father's gens, but he may also acquire his mother's gens. By marriage he always acquires the prerogatives of his wife's family. It is only here that such prerogatives are connected with the gentes. They refer generally to the use of masks and certain ceremonies of the winter dance, the most important of which is the Hā'mats'a, the man-biter. But the accession to these privileges is not only a right of the young man, it is also his duty to accept them. Among the Salish tribes of the Gulf of Georgia the division into gentes is not as clearly defined as farther north. Here a group of gentes forms a tribe, each gens inhabiting one village. In removing the village from one place to the other they retain the same name, which, however, is not the name of the people, properly speaking, but that of their village. Each gens derives its origin from a single man who descended from heaven, and whose sons and grandsons became the ancestors of the gens, the child always belonging to his father's gens. While among the northern tribes marriages

in the same gens, or phratry, are strictly prohibited, there exists no such
law among the Salish.

I have not found any trace of a division into gentes among the
Kutonaqa.

MYTHOLOGY.

It is one of the most interesting problems of ethnology to study the
development of a system of mythology. On the north-west coast of
America this study is the more interesting, as we can show how legends
migrated from tribe to tribe. The great hero of the mythology of the
northern tribes is the raven, who created daylight, mountains, trees, men.
These raven legends have spread very far south, being even known to
the Cowitchin of Vancouver Island, and probably still farther south.
The hero of the mythology of the southern tribes, on the other hand, is
the great wanderer, the son of the deity, who, on his migrations all over
the world, transformed men into animals, and animals into men. It
appears that this legend, which is known from the mouth of the Columbia
to Bella Bella, originated with the Salish tribes; however, we do not
know how far it extends inland. Another legend belonging to these
tribes has spread far north. It refers to a visit to heaven, and the marriage of a young man to the sun's daughter. Traces of this tale are
found among the Tsimshian. The myths of the Kutona'qa and of the
Okanagan refer principally to the coyote. I shall proceed to describe
briefly the myths of the various tribes, at the same time pointing out
their connection among each other.

The Tlingit say that the world was originally swinging to and fro in
space. There was something underneath it that was to serve as a rest
for the world; the latter approached it, but never succeeded in joining it.
All animals tried in vain to fasten the world to it. At last a female
spirit, Harishanc'kō (=the woman under us), smeared her belly with deer
tallow, lay down under the world, and when the latter approached the
underworld again the tallow fastened both together. The earth is considered square, the corners pointing north, south, east, and west. In the
north there is an enormous hole into which the water of the ocean gushes,
and from which it returns, thus causing the tides. There is another idea,
to the effect that the world is sharp like a knife's edge, but this seems to
be said more in a moral aspect, the meaning being that the road of right
doing is narrow; whoever does wrong falls from the road and dies. The
earth rests on Harishanc'kō, and when the latter moves there is an earth-
quake. The moon is the sun's husband. There is a chief in heaven
called Tahi't, the ruler of those who fall in war. These fighting souls
produce the aurora. It is worth remarking that this belief is also found
among the Eskimo. On the same level with the earth, but outside its
borders, is the country of those who died of sickness.

The creation legend of the Tlingit is as follows:—In the beginning
there lived a great chief and his sister. The chief killed all his sister's
sons as soon as they were born. One day when the woman went to the
beach mourning the death of her children, a seagull advised her to swallow
three stones. She obeyed, and after a few days gave birth to three boys,
the oldest of whom was Yētl, the raven. He wanted to avenge the death
of his brothers, and challenged his uncle. The latter tried to drown Yētl
by making the waters rise until the whole earth was covered. He kept
himself afloat by means of his hat, which grew higher as the waters were

rising. Yĕtl, however, flew up to the sky, and at last pressed down his uncle's hat, thus drowning his enemy. The waters disappeared again, and then Yĕtl obtained the sun, which was in possession of a chief, and the fresh water, which was owned by the fabulous K·anŭ'k·. He made trees and mountains next, and finally tried to create man. First he shaped human figures out of stone and wood, but did not succeed. Then he made man out of grass, and for this reason men are mortal. After this Yĕtl began to wander all over the world, and in all his further adventures he is described as extremely voracious and greedy.

The mythology of the Haida is substantially the same as that of the Tlingit. The raven is called Yĕtl by the Kaigani, while on Queen Charlotte Island his name is Qoia. His uncle's name is Nenkyilstla's.

The Tsimshian have also traditions referring to the raven, but he is not considered the creator of men. They consider the Nass River region as their original home, and the Nass language the oldest dialect of the Tsimshian. The origin of men is thus accounted for :—A long time ago a rock and an elder, near the mouth of Nass River, were about to give birth to men. The children of the elder were the first to be born, therefore man is mortal. If the children of the rock had been born first, he would have been immortal. From the rock, however, he received the nails on hands and feet.

The Tsimshian worship the deity in heaven, Leqa', who lives above the sun. The raven myths were evidently imported from some foreign sources, and then the raven was made the descendant of this deity in order to account for his supernatural powers. This legend, which is found from Nass river as far south as the northern portion of Vancouver Island, is substantially as follows :—A chief's wife, who was with child, died and was buried. In the grave she gave birth to a boy, who grew up feeding upon his mother's body. Eventually he was discovered and claimed by the chief, who grew to be very fond of him. The boy used to shoot birds and to skin them. One day he put on a bird's skin and flew up to heaven, where he married the deity's daughter. They had a son, who, when born, dropped from his mother's hand and fell into the ocean. He was found by a chief, and in course of time became Tqĕmsem, of whom the same adventures are told which Yĕtl is said to have accomplished. He appears generally in the shape of the raven.

The flood, of which the Tsimshian also tell, is said to have been sent by heaven as a punishment for the ill-behaviour of man. First, all people, with the exception of a few, were destroyed by a flood, and later on by fire. Before the flood the earth was not as it is now, but there were no mountains and no trees. After the flood Leqa' created these too. The earth is considered to be round, and resting on a pillar that is held by an old woman.

The most important of the Kwākiutl legends is that of the wanderer K·ā'nikila. He is the son of the deity, and descended from heaven to earth, where he was born again of a woman. When he came to be grown up he wandered all over the world, transforming his enemies into animals and making friends with many a mighty chief. Another important legend is that of the mink, Tlĕ'selakila (meaning the son of the sun), who made a chain of arrows reaching from the sky to the earth, on which he climbed up and visited his father, who let him carry the sun in his stead. When, however, he went too fast, and set the earth on fire, his father cast him into the sea. While the northern tribes of this race are acquainted with the raven legends, those farther south ascribe all the adventures of the raven to the mink. Another class of legends of the Kwākiutl is of great importance as referring to the spirits of the dances. I will mention in this place that these remarkable dances have evidently originated with the Kwākiutl, although they are at present practised by the Tsimshian and Haida, and by some of the southern tribes. The Tsimshian practise only a few of them, the names of the dances being all of Kwākiutl origin. According to their own statements they were obtained by intermarriage with the Hēiltsuk. The Haida adopted them from the Tsimshian. In all these dances ornaments of cedar bark, dyed red, are used, and it appears that this custom also originated among the Kwākiutl. The most prominent figure of this winter dance is the man-eater, called Hā'mats'a (the eater) by the Kwākiutl, Elaqō'tla by the Bilqula, Ō'lala by the Haida and Tsimshian. The latter call his dance also the Wīhalai't (the great dance). The Hā'mats'a is initiated by a spirit, referring to which numerous traditions exist. It is a peculiarity of Kwākiutl mythology that it treats of many supernatural beings, while farther north almost exclusively the heaven, the sun, moon, and raven have supernatural power. Among these beings the following are of importance:—The Tsōnō'k·oa (probably a mythical form of the grizzly bear), the Thunderbird, the Si'siutl (the double-headed snake), and a cuttlefish of enormous size. The myths of the Hēiltsuk are much influenced by those of the Bilqula, their eastern neighbours.

The legends of the Nutka treat also principally of the great wanderer, and embody, so far as I am aware, no element which is not found among the Kwākiutl.

The legends of the Salish vary to a great extent among the various tribes, those of the coast tribes resembling the myths of the Kwākiutl. The wanderer and the sun are here the heroes of the greater part of the myths. The legend of the wanderer does not differ from that of the Kwākiutl, except in that he is himself the deity. Each remarkable stone or rock is described as being a man transformed by him. He made a great fire in order to destroy man, and later on made the ocean rise and cover the land. The ascent to heaven on a chain of arrows is one of the principal objects of their legends, the tale treating frequently of a murder of the old sun and the origin of the new one. Besides this, the double-headed snake is of importance, even more so than among the Kwākiutl.

The mythology of the Bilqula, whose language is closely related to that of the dialects of the Gulf of Georgia, differs greatly from that of the other Salish tribes, being evidently influenced by their neighbours. Their mythology, on the other hand, has influenced that of the Hēiltsuk. I do not think that the wanderer legend is found among them. They tell of the raven who created daylight, and of two men, Masmasalā'niq and Yula'timot, who descended from heaven, created man, and gave him his arts. This legend is one of the most beautiful of those found on the coast. Its origin is doubtful. It would be necessary to study the mythology of the tribes of the interior more closely in order to arrive at a satisfactory understanding of this myth. The Bilqula have also the legend of the mink carrying the sun. They call him T'ōtk·on'ya.

I am not well acquainted with the myths of the tribes of the interior, having collected only a limited number among the Ntlakapamuq. They also tell of the wanderer who transformed men into stones, but it is doubtful whether he is in any way connected with the deity. Their legends referring to the sun are numerous, one of the most important being the visit to the sun. There are many legends referring to the raven and to the mink, and here for the first time we find the coyote playing an important part in the mythology.

The heroes of the myths of the Kutonāqa are the sun and the coyote. These myths are more closely connected with those of their south-eastern neighbours than with those of the north-west coast Indians. It is, however, of interest to notice that the legend of a chain of arrows reaching up to the sky, and a conquest of the sky, which is so important in the Salish tales, occurs here also. One of the most interesting legends is that of the origin of the sun. The animals tried by turns to act as the sun, but none succeeded. The coyote almost succeeded, but as he made it too hot, and as he told everything he saw going on upon the earth, he was also compelled to give up his place in the sky, and then the two sons of the lynx became sun and moon. Later on, the coyote became the father-in-law of the sun, and many are the tales that refer to his adventures. He plays a part similar to that of the raven in the tales of the Tlingit.

RELIGION, SHAMANISM, MORTUARY CUSTOMS.

A study of mythology and of customs shows that the Indians of this province worshipped principally the sun or the heaven. The Tlingit and Haida pray to the moon, and in praying blow feathers up as an offering. They also pray to mountains, and believe that the animals of their crest protect them, although they are not forbidden to kill them. They believe in the transmigration of souls, the soul of the deceased being born again in a child of the same gens. The souls of animals return in the same way in their young. Sickness is to a great extent ascribed to witchcraft, and it is the duty of the shaman to cure the sick and to find out the witch. The shaman is initiated by acquiring a spirit. Cleanliness is considered as being agreeable to the spirits; therefore the novice must bathe frequently. Great powers are ascribed to people who abstained from sexual intercourse. The dead, except shamans, are burned, and the ashes put up in small boxes. Shamans are buried near the beach, one coffin being deposited on top of the other.

The Tsimshian have a supreme deity called Leqa'. Prayers are frequently not addressed to him directly, but to spirits, the Neqno'q, who convey them to him. Most of the prayers have conventional forms. In praying for clear weather for instance, they say: ' Neqno'q, Neqno'q, chief, chief, have mercy! Look down upon thy people under thee. Pull up thy foot and wipe thy face!' They think that the existence of man is pleasing to the deity, and that he enjoys the smoke rising from their fires. They pray: ' Have mercy upon us! Else there will be nobody to make the smoke rise up to thee. Have pity upon us!' The Tsimshian believe that the dead live in a country similar to our own, and that they are never in want. The dead are buried, but the heart is taken out and buried apart. Chiefs are sometimes burnt, and so are shamans. If a series of deaths occurred in a family, the mourners used to cut off the first joint of the fourth finger, in order to put an end to the misfortunes of their family.

The Kwākintl worship the sun. It is not quite clear whether they worship K'anikila, the wanderer, besides, or whether they address their prayers only to the sun. Their dances are closely connected with their

religious ideas, particularly the dance Tlok·oala (= something unexpected
coming from above), which, in course of time, has partly been adopted by
all their neighbours.   There are a great number of spirits of this dance,
each of which has his own class of shamans, the duties and prerogatives
of whom vary according to the character of their genii.   The Kwäkintl
bury their dead in boxes, which are placed in small houses or on trees.
Posts, carved according to the crest of the deceased, are placed in front
of the graves.   Food is burnt for the dead on the beach.   Their mourning
ceremonies are very complicated and rigorous.

The Coast Salish worship the sun.   They pray to him and are not
allowed to take their morning meal until the day is well advanced.   The
wanderer, called Kumanō'otl by the Comox, Qäls by the Cowitchin and
Lkungen, and Qäis by the Skqomish, is also worshipped.   They believe
that he lives in heaven and loves the good, but punishes the bad.   The
art of shamanism was bestowed by him upon the first man, who brought
it down from heaven.

The Kutonäqa are also sun-worshippers, even more decidedly so than
any of the other tribes.   They pray to the sun.   They offer him a smoke
from their pipe before smoking themselves, and sacrifice their eldest
children in order to secure prosperity to their families.   They believe
that the souls of the deceased go towards the east, and will return in
course of time with the sun.   Occasionally they have great festivals,
during which they expect the return of the dead.   They have also the
custom of cutting off the first joints of the fingers as a sacrifice to the
sun.   They pierce their breasts and arms with sharp needles and cut off
pieces of flesh, which they offer to the sun.   It is doubtful whether
they practise the sun-dance of their eastern neighbours.   The dead are
buried, their heads facing the east.   It is of interest that the positions of
the body after death are considered to be prophetic of future events.
The mourners cut their hair and bury it with the deceased.   Warriors
are buried among trees which are peeled and painted red.   Each shaman
has his own genius, generally a bird or another animal, which he acquires
by fasting in the woods or on the mountains.   The shamans are able to
speak with the souls of absent or deceased persons, and are skilful
jugglers.

Report on the Sarcee Indians, by the Rev. E. F. Wilson.

The Sarcee Indians belong to the great Athabascan or Tinneh stock,
to which the Chipewyans, Beavers, Hares, and others in the North-West
and, it is said, the Navajoes, in New Mexico, also belong.   They were
formerly a powerful nation, but are now reduced to a few hundreds.
Their reserve, which consists of a fine tract of prairie land, about a
hundred square miles in extent, adjoins that of the Blackfeet, in Alberta,
a little south of the Canadian Pacific Railway line, and seventy or eighty
miles east of the Rocky Mountains.   Although friendly and formerly
confederate with the Blackfeet, they bear no affinity to that people; they
belong to a distinct stock and speak an altogether different language.
They are divided into two bands—the Blood Sarcees and the Real
Sarcees.

During my visit, which lasted seven days, I had several interviews
with their chief, ' Bull's Head,' a tall, powerful man, about sixty years of
age ; and it was from him and one or two of his leading men that I

gathered most of my information. I found, however, that the Sarcees were not so ready to converse, or to tell either about their language or their history, as were the Blackfeet, whom I visited last summer. Tea and tobacco seemed to be with them the chief desiderata, and except with gifts of this kind it seemed almost impossible to gain anything from them. And after all, even when plied with these commodities, the information they gave was very meagre, and often far from satisfactory. From what little I saw of these people I should be inclined to say that they are of a lower order and inferior in mental capacity to the Blackfeet; I judge this chiefly by the style in which they told their stories and traditions, such as they were, and by their having no elaborated theories as to certain phenomena in nature, about which many other of the Indian tribes have always so much to say.

Chief ' Bull's Head,' in reply to my questions as to their early history, made a great show of oratory, both by voice and gesture, but much of what he said was very childish and confused, and seemed to be scarcely worth the trouble of putting down.

These people call the Blackfeet ' Katee,' the Crees ' Nishinna,' the Sioux ' Kaispa,' and themselves ' Soténnă.' The Indians of their own stock, as I understand, they call ' Tinnätte.' These two last names seem certainly to connect them with the great ' Tinneh ' or Athabascan nation. Sarcee (or rather Sarxi) is the name by which they are called by the Blackfeet.

WHENCE THESE PEOPLE CAME.

' Formerly,' said ' Bull's Head,' ' the Sarcee territory extended from the Rocky Mountains to the Big River (either the Saskatchewan or the Peace River). Our delight was to make corrals for the buffaloes, and to drive them over the cut bank and let them fall. Those were glorious days, when we could mount our swift-footed horses, and ride like the wind after the flying herd ; but now the buffalo is gone we hang our heads, we are poor. And then, too, we used to fight those liars, the Crees : we engaged in many a bloody battle, and their bullets pierced our teepees. Thirty battles have I seen. When I was a child the Sarcees were in number like the grass ; the Blackfeet and Bloods and Peigans were as nothing in comparison. Battles with the Crees and disease brought in among us by the white man have reduced us to our present pitiable state.'

Another Indian told us how the Sarcees were at one time one people with the Chipewyans, and gave us the myth which accounts for their separation. ' Formerly,' he said, ' we lived in the north country. We were many thousands in number. We were travelling south. It was winter, and we had to cross a big lake on the ice. There was an elk's horn sticking out of the ice. A squaw went and struck the horn with an axe. The elk raised himself from the ice and shook his head. The people were all frightened and ran away. Those that ran toward the north became the Chipewyans, and we who ran toward the south are the " Soténnă " or " Sarcees." '

' The Chipewyans,' said ' Bull's Head,' ' speak our language. It is twenty years since I saw a Chipewyan. We call them " Teohtin." They live up north, beyond the Big River ' (probably the Peace River).

Their Traditions, Beliefs, &c.

' There was a time,' said ' Bull's Head,' ' when there were no lakes.
The lakes and rivers were occasioned by the bursting of the belly of the
buffalo. It was when the belly of the buffalo burst that the people
divided; some went to the north and some to the south. For years and
years I have been told that the Creator made all people, and I believe it.
I have heard my mother and other old people speak of the days when
there were no guns and no horses, when our people had only arrows,
and had to hunt the buffalo on foot; that must have been a very long
time ago.'

The Sarcees have a tradition similar to that of the Blackfeet about
men and women being first made separately, and then being brought
together through the action of the mythical being ' Napiw.'

They have also a tradition of the flood, which accords in its main
features with that of the Ojibways, Crees, and other Canadian tribes.
They say that when the world was flooded there were only one man and
one woman left, and these two saved themselves on a raft, on which they
also collected animals and birds of all sorts. The man sent a beaver
down to dive and it brought up a little mud from the bottom, and this
the man moulded in his hands to form a new world. At first the world
was so small that a little bird could walk round it, but it kept getting
bigger and bigger. ' First,' said the narrator, ' our father took up his
abode on it, then there were men, then women, then animals, then birds.
Our father then created the rivers, the mountains, the trees, and all the
things as we now see them.'

When the story was finished I told the narrator that the Ojibway
tradition was very much the same as theirs, only that they said it was a
musk-rat that brought up the earth and not a beaver. Upon this five or
six of the men who were squatting around inside the teepee smoking
cried, ' Yes, yes! The man has told you lies; it was a musk-rat, it was
a musk-rat! '

It seems dubious whether the Sarcees are sun-worshippers; but, like
the Blackfeet, they call the sun ' our father,' and the earth ' our mother.'
They also engage each summer in the ' sun-dance.' They depend also for
guidance in their actions on signs in the sky and on dreams. They think
they know when there is going to be a fight by the appearance of the
moon. One of their number, named ' Many Swans,' says he is going to
have a good crop this year, for he dreamed that a white woman came
down from above and asked to see his garden, and he showed his garden
to the woman, and it was all green.

' Bull's Head ' had no theory to give as to the cause of thunder; he
knew that Indians of other tribes said it was a big bird flapping its
wings, but his people did not say so; they did not know what it was;
neither had they anything to say about an eclipse.

Manner of Living.

The Sarcee Indians are at present all pagans; they appear to have no
liking for the white people, and the white people seem to have little
liking for them, and would gladly deprive them of their lands and drive
them away farther into the wilderness were they permitted to do so.
But the paternal Government, as represented by the Indian Department,

takes care that they are not imposed upon. There is an Indian Agent stationed on their reserve, who twice a week doles out to them the Government rations, consisting of excellent fresh beef and good flour; and there is also a farm instructor, who has charge of the farming stock and implements, and does what he can to induce these warriors and hunters to farm.

They have also residing among them a missionary of the Church of England, who visits them in their teepees, and does his best to collect their little blanketed children to school, giving two Government biscuits to each scholar as a reward for attendance. But the people are evidently averse to all these things, which are being done for their good. Their only idea of the white man seems to be that of a trespassing individual, who has more in his possession than he knows what to do with, and may therefore fairly be preyed upon.

The dress of these people consists, as with other wild Indians, of a breech-clout, a pair of blanket leggings, beaded moccasins, and a blanket thrown loosely, but gracefully, over one or both shoulders. They wear their long black hair in plaits, hanging vertically, one plait on each side of the face, and one or more at the back. Some of them knot their hair on the top of the head; and some, I noticed, wore a coloured handkerchief folded and tied round the temples. This, I believe, is one distinguishing mark of the Navajo Indians in New Mexico. Very often the leggings and moccasins are dispensed with, and the man appears to have nothing on except his grey, white, or coloured blanket. The women wear an ordinary woman's dress of rough make and material, and short in the skirt, next to the skin, leggings and moccasins, and a blanket round the shoulders. Ornaments are worn by both sexes, but chiefly by the men. They consist of brooches and earrings made of steel, necklaces and bracelets made of bright coloured beads, bones, claws, teeth, and brass wire, and finger-rings, also of brass wire, coiled ten or twelve times, and covering the lower joint of the finger. Every finger of each hand is sometimes covered with these rings. Both men and women paint the upper part of the face with ochre or vermilion. The people live in 'teepees,' conical-shaped lodges, made of poles covered with tent cotton, in the summer, and in low log huts, plastered over with mud, in winter. They depend for their subsistence almost entirely on the rations supplied by Government. They keep numbers of ponies, but seem to make little use of them beyond riding about. They keep no cattle or animals of any kind beyond their ponies and dogs. The latter are savage, and are said to be descendants of the wolf and the coyote, with which animals they still often breed. They seem to have no manufactures; they make no canoes, baskets, &c., but they know how to prepare the hides and skins of the animals they kill, and they make their own clothing, saddles, bows and arrows, and moccasins. Some of the women do very excellent bead-work. Bridles they do not use; a rope or thong fastened to the pony's lower jaw takes the place of a bridle; their whips are a short stout stick, studded with brass nails, and provided with two leathern thongs as lashes at one end, and a loop for the wrist at the other. Their bows are of cherry wood, strung with a leathern thong, and their arrows of the Saskatoon willow, winged with feathers, and pointed with scrap-iron, filed to a sharp point. The shaft of the arrow has four shallow grooves down its entire length.

Gambling.

The Sarcees, like most other wild Indians, are inveterate gamblers. They will gamble everything away—ponies, teepees, blankets, leggings, moccasins—till they have nothing left but their breech-clout. In my report of the Blackfeet last year I mentioned the use of a little hoop or wheel for gambling purposes. I find that the Sarcees also use this, and two of them showed me how they play the game. A little piece of board, if procurable, or two or three flattened sticks, laid one on the other, are put for a target, at a distance of eighteen or twenty feet from the starting-point, and the two players then take their places beside each other; one has the little wheel in his left hand, an arrow in his right; the other one has only an arrow. The play is to roll the wheel and to deliver the two arrows simultaneously, all aiming at the mark which has been set up. If the wheel falls over on one of the arrows, it counts so many points, according to the number of beads on the wire spoke of the wheel that touch the arrow. Nothing is counted unless the little wheel falls on one of the arrows. The articles for which they play are valued at so many points each. A blanket is worth, perhaps, ten points, a pony fifty, and so on.

Another method by which these people gamble is as follows : Two men squat side by side on the ground, with a blanket over their knees, and they have some small article, such as two or three brass beads tied together, which they pass from one to another under the blanket; and the other side, which also consists of two persons, has to guess in which hand the article is to be found—very much like our children's ' hunt the whistle.' The Sarcees use also the English playing cards, but it is a game of their own that they play with them. Whoever gets the most cards is the winner.

Matrimony.

The Sarcees are polygamous, the men having two, three, or four wives. The time of moving camp is generally looked upon as a propitious time for love-making. The camp is in the form of a ring, with the horses picketed in the centre. Early in the morning the young men drive the horses to a swamp or slough to water them. They are thinking, perhaps, of some young squaw whom they wish to approach, but they are ashamed to speak to her. Then, as soon as all is ready for the move, the chief gives the word, and the callers summon the people to start on the march. The chief goes first and leads the way. Now is the opportunity for the bashful young swains; they drop behind the rest and manage to ride alongside the young women of their choice, and to get a few words into their ears. If the young woman approves the offer, she follows her white sister's example by referring the young man to her parents. If the parents consent, mutual presents are exchanged, such as horses, blankets, &c.; the girl is dressed in her best, and her face painted, and the young man takes her away. A husband can divorce himself from his wife at any time if he pleases, but he has to restore the presents that he received with her, or their equivalent. Girls are often betrothed at ten years of age and married at fourteen. A betrothed girl may not look in a man's face until after her marriage. A man may not meet his mother-in-law; if he chance to touch her accidentally he must give her a present. At a feast among the Blackfeet at which I was present an impatient mother-in-law was standing without and sending messages to the son-in-law within to make haste and leave before all the good things were done, so that she might come in and get her share; but he sent word back that he was in no hurry. Parents do not often punish their children, but sometimes, in a fit of ill-temper, will beat them cruelly. They are more cruel to their wives than to their children. While I was making these notes a Sarcee woman came into the lodge with her nose cut off; her husband had done it as a punishment for her keeping company with another man.

MEDICINE.

The Sarcees are not considered to be much versed in the use of medicinal roots and herbs; they are much more ready to take the white man's medicine than are their neighbours, the Blackfeet.

Among themselves they depend chiefly on magic and witchcraft for recovery from sickness. There are about a dozen so-called 'medicinemen' in the camp, but most of them are *women*. Chief among them is an old squaw named 'Good Lodge.' They are always highly paid for their services, whether the patient recovers or not. A medicine-man when called in to see a sick person will first make a stone red-hot in the fire, then touch the stone with his finger, and with the same finger press various parts of the patient's body, to ascertain the locality and character of the sickness. Then he will suck the place vigorously and keep spitting the disease (so he pretends) from his mouth. This is accompanied by drum beating and shaking a rattle. The Sarcees do not bleed or cup, but they blister (often quite efficaciously) by applying the end of a piece of burning touchwood to the affected part. They also use the vapour-bath. To do this a little bower, about three feet high, is made of pliable green sticks, covered over closely with blankets. Several stones are heated red and placed in a small hole in the ground inside the bower; and over these the patient sits in a state of nudity and keeps putting water on the stones, which is supplied to him by an attendant from without. When thoroughly steamed, and almost boiled, he rushes out, and plunges into cold water. This treatment sometimes effects a cure, but more often induces bad results and death. The vapour-bath, as above described, is used very extensively by Indians of many different tribes; some, however, omit the plunge into cold water.

BURIAL CUSTOMS.

I had a good opportunity to investigate the burial customs of these people. Riding across the prairie with a young Englishman who had spent several years in the neighbourhood, we came upon a 'bluff,' or small copse, of fir and poplar trees, covering some two or three acres of ground. We suspected it was a burial-ground, and, dismounting from our horses, entered it. No sooner had we done so than we found ourselves in the midst of the dead—the bodies wound up in blankets and tent-cloth, like mummies, and deposited on scaffolds from six to eight feet from the ground. Four or five of these bodies could be seen from one point, and others became visible as we pushed our way through the tangled underbrush. A little baby's body, wrapped up in cloth, was jammed into the forked branch of a fir tree about five-and-a-half feet from the ground. The earth was black and boggy and the stench nauseous. Here and there lay the bleached bones and tangled manes of ponies that had been shot when their warrior owners died—the idea being that the equine spirits would accompany the deceased persons to the other world, and make themselves useful there. Beside each body lay a bundle of earthly goods—blankets, leggings, saddles, &c., also cups, tin pots, kettles, and everything that the spirit of the departed could be supposed to want. Pursuing our explorations we came upon a 'death teepee.' I had heard of these, and had often desired to see one. It was just an ordinary teepee, or Indian lodge, made of poles leaning from the edge of a circle, fifteen feet or so in diameter, to a point at the top, and covered with common tent cloth. The stench was disgusting, and the ground like a cesspool; but I wanted to see all, so we effected an entrance and examined the contents. The old warrior, whoever he may have been, was wrapped up in rotting, sodden blankets, sitting with his back against an ordinary Indian back-rest. We could not see his face, as the blanket covered it, but the top of his scalp was visible and a great bunch of slimy, filthy-looking eagle feathers adorned his head; just behind him hung his leathern quiver, ornamented with a leathern fringe, two feet in length and full of arrows; also his beaded tobacco pouch; and by his side were a tin basin, a fire-blackened tin pot with a cover, and a large bundle of blankets, clothing, and other effects. I made a hasty sketch of the dismal scene and then retired. We were glad to mount our horses once more and to breathe again the fresh air of the prairie.

PHYSICAL DEVELOPMENT.

The Sarcees do not strike me as so fine or tall a race as the Blackfeet, although one whose measure I here give was of about the same height as the Blackfoot Indian, 'Boy Chief,' whom I measured last year. They have remarkably small hands and feet. I traced on paper the hand of a Sarcee Indian named 'Head above Water.'

Following is the measurement of an adult Sarcee, about thirty years of age, named 'Many Shields.'

		ft.	in.
1.	Height from ground to vertex[1]	5	$8\frac{1}{4}$
2.	" " meatus auditorius	5	$3\frac{1}{4}$
3.	" " chin	4	$11\frac{1}{8}$
5.	" " umbilicus	3	$5\frac{3}{8}$
7.	" " fork	2	8
8.	" " knee-cap joint	1	$8\frac{1}{8}$
11.	" " elbow (bent)	3	$6\frac{1}{2}$
12.	" " tip of finger (hanging vertically)	2	$2\frac{1}{4}$
13.	Height—sitting on the ground	2	$11\frac{1}{4}$
16.	Circumference of chest at armpits	3	0
17.	" " mammæ	2	$11\frac{1}{4}$
18.	" at haunches	2	$11\frac{1}{2}$
26.	Span—outstretched arms	5	$8\frac{1}{4}$
27.	" thumb to middle finger	0	$7\frac{1}{2}$
28.	Length of thumb	0	$2\frac{1}{8}$
29.	" foot	0	$9\frac{3}{4}$
30.	Head—greatest circumference (over glabella)	1	$11\frac{1}{2}$
31.	" arc, root of nose to inion	1	4
32.	" " meatus auditorius, over head	1	$1\frac{3}{4}$
33.	" " over glabella to meatus auditorius	1	1
41.	" length of face, root of nose to chin	0	$5\frac{1}{4}$

Hair, eyes, and skin the same as those of the Blackfoot Indian 'Boy Chief' (see Report of 1887).

[1] In the measurements of the Blackfoot 'Boy Chief,' given in the Report of last year, the 'height from ground to vertex' should have been 5 ft. $8\frac{3}{4}$ in., instead of 4 ft. $8\frac{3}{4}$ in., as printed.

Two or three young Indians. tried the strength of their eyesight. They could count the prescribed dots at a distance of 28 feet.

LANGUAGE.

I cannot give as full a report of the Sarcee language as I did of the Blackfoot, for the reason that no one, so far as I could learn, outside the Sarcee tribe has any knowledge of it. The missionary in charge had only arrived a few weeks before, and though he knew the Blackfoot, and through that medium could make himself understood by a few of the people, he knew nothing whatever of Sarcee. We were told that it was an exceedingly difficult language to acquire, and full of gutturals; others said that it had no vowels in it; others that it was like a hen cackling. Under these circumstances it was vain to expect to make out the grammatical rules of the language, but I thought I would do what I could to collect a small vocabulary of words. A few of the people understood Blackfoot, and some few others Cree, and through the medium of these two languages I was able to collect the following Sarcee words and short sentences:—

VOCABULARY.

Pronounce *a* and *ă* as the first and second *a* in larva, *e* as in they, *i* as in pique, *ĭ* as in pick, *o* as in note, *u* as in rule, *ai* as in aisle, *au* as ou in bough, *ḥ* guttural as in *ich* (German), *ĝ* (a sound found also in the Sioux language) pronounced like the Arabic *ghain*, a *ghr* sound; *tc* like *ch* in church, *ñ* like the French nasal *n* in *bon*.

man (or men)	kăttini	a big man	kăttini tcu
woman	tsikă'	women	tsikuá
boy	sittă	boys	sittămika
girl	ctráka		
infant	tsittă		
my, thy, his father	ittrá, nittrá, mittrá		
my mother	inná	my son	siĝá
thy son	niĝála	Bull's Head's son	ilgătsi măĝála
elder brother	kiniĝá	younger brother	nish'itla
Indians (prairie people),	tklukodissána		
Indians (probably of Tinne nation),	Tinn'átte		
my head	sitsitsi'n	thy head	nitsits'ina
Bull's Head's head	ilgátsi mitsitsina		
my eye	sinnăĝa'	my nose	sitsi
my arm	s'ikamuă	my leg	sigăs
my, thy, his hand	s'illa, nĭlla, milla		
my foot	sikkă	my heart	sitsánnăĝă
my blood	sittikla	town	natsiĝan'iklăte
chief	hak'itci	my friend	klóssă
house	nátsiga	a small house	natsiga sitla
teepee	kauwă	kettle	missokólilli
tinpot	ăsrá	small ditto	ăsrá sítla
basin	tcistlă	axe	tsĭlh
knife	măs	my knife	sim'ăssa
thy knife	nim'ăssa	his knife	măskisklă
boat	tăn'ikăss'i	moccasin	naka
boot	kásteagé	pipe [pouch	mĭstoté
tobacco	katcĭn	his tobacco	natisgáni kisklă
sun	tcătrá	moon	inaĝa

English	Native	English	Native
star	soli	day	tsinnis
night	itlăggé	spring	tagganăgă
summer	hatakòsi	autumn	hă'ssini
winter	sússkăbe	next winter	klikă sásskăbe
last winter (snow)	tanatsósosáte	it is snowing	sosáte
the wind is blowing	tikăn'istci	it is cold	koskáss
it is warm	kákow'iskis	it is raining	tcaté
fire	koli	water	tuh
earth	nĭlka	river	s'iska
lake	totcu	well or spring	hat'ăllălĭlĭ
prairie	tklùka	the RockyMoun-	tca
island	no	stone [tains	tsa
tree	itci	a pine tree	kah
a big tree	itci tcu	a small tree	itci sitla
wood	ditsiá	a log of wood	ntisseá
brushwood	titci	grass	kutló
meat, flesh	ăl'ină	dog, klih	dogs, klikah
horse	isklih	horses	isklikah
my dog	sĭlltsa klih	my dog or horse	sil'itsa
mare	isklih hănimaká	my mare	hănimaká sil'itsa
ox	haidéklishi	cow	hănimaká haideklishi
buffalo	hănni	buffaloes	hannile
a black ox	haidéklishi, di'skăshi		
deer	kuini	elk	tcáse
the black elk	ádidinidjé	rabbit	nikla'tila
snake	natósăgă	bird	ilkáğe
egg	iğasa	duck	tces
fish	klúka	pig (big dog)	kliká tcu
gun	sittrăna	cart	măssèklăshi
book	djinishă	hat	sitsin'it ila
coat	dilkoshi	handkerchief	sili'ssităniga
trousers	istlá	leggings	isttăkok'ita
shirt	kitcistaniă	blanket	tc'iyisi-tcastcide
flour	netsokăssi	yes	a
paper	tătklishi	no	itsi'tawa
money	diltilih	one	àgligah (klikkazah)
whip	istláhiklá	two	akiye (ăkinnă)
red	dilgăssé	three	trănki (traanah)
white	dig'assigă	four	didji (dizhná)
black	dishkoshó	five	kosita
God (the Creator)	isklúni	six	kostranni
„ (our Father)	nătuninan	seven	tcistcidi
devil	sinómato'ikli	eight	clashdédji
heaven	tsclaráh	nine	klăkuhigá
minister	dikăhatsi dikalá	ten	kúnisnăñ
soldier	trăskilláh	eleven	kli'kkunitañ
big	tcu	twelve	akámităñ
small	sitlá	thirteen	trágimitañ
strong	magánisis'ta	fourteen	didjimitañ
old	tcanăte	fifteen	wiltăñmitañ
it is good	mókaƀilli	sixteen	wistañmitañ
it is not good	mátogúgli	seventeen	tcistimitan
„ „ „	tósăma	eighteen	clashdédjimitañ
he is dead"	trásitsá	nineteen	klikunäñmitañ
this	tcigé	twenty	ak'ădde
that	tetegéla	twenty-one	akădde egligimitañ
all	kănniltăla	twenty-two	„ ckámitañ
many	niklá	twenty-three	„ ctrañkimitañ
who is it ?	mataganita ?	twenty-four	„ edijimitañ
far off	kússá	thirty	trañte
near	willoá	forty	pisde
here	tătigè	fifty	kositáté
there	niugúte	sixty	kóstrăté

what is that?	tatáita? tata .?	seventy	t'cisteidí'nni
yesterday	ilkhá	eighty	elasìdedjde
to-morrow	nákkoolikái or eklátsi	ninety	klakúhidinnã
white man	dikábãlli	one hundred	konisnãñte
American	mãm'ãssi-nitsãnã	I walk	sinna nìshelkh
I	sinni, sinna . . .	thou walkest	ninna kiyelkh
thou	ninn'ila, ninna . . .	he walks	yiyelkh
he	àtigan'itta, in'ila	I am asleep	sinna nista
they	kisãhãtai	he is asleep	sitti
thou art asleep	ninna nitta		

Is it your knife?	ni mãssã lãh ?
I love him	sinna tsit tó midisi
you love him	ninna tsit tó midininni
he loves him	tsitto midininni
I love it	tsitto midisi
I do not love it	totsitto midisi
two men	ãkiye k'ãttini
two women	ãk'iye tsikúah
one dog	klih klikazah
the boy runs	sittá kañilkla
the dog runs	klih kañilkla
the dogs run	klikah nilkla (?)
one dog runs	klih klikazah nilkla
I run	sinha kaniskla
thou runnest	ninna ékanilkla
he runs	kanilkla
we	eklitãnilkla
I arrive	sinha nãnìshrã
thon	ninna enãñicilá
he	iñiila enãnikãtilã
we	nãnie nãnìðigãltik (?)
they	kisãluãta nãniésãlìñeila or nanãltãltila (?)
he rides	klikadiskla
I smoke	siðiisto
you smoke	niniito
he smokes	itotila (or does he smoke ?)
the Blackfoot smokes	katci itótila
we smoke	isáitótila
they smoke	àtótila
I smoked yesterday	ilkha siñiistóte
I shall smoke to-morrow	eklátsi sin itá isto
he will smoke to-morrow	eklátsi itá isto
I will look for them to-morrow	eklatsi makògidisi
I drive them home	nanìshó
if he goes he will see you	itsitíya ti istea
if I go you will see me	ni'sitíya ti nistea
king, big chief	Akìtsi nakáwa
go home	nãtishú
come in	kunã
my house is good	sahokókãñilli
my horses are good	silíteikãkonilli
it is not good	to mãkanilli
give it to me	sahanãha (or tãstóa)
he gave it to me	sahanahã
come here	tãst'iyã
be quick	a wãt tã
do not be afraid	to nãnna nìdji
I am hungry	sitsã'ãñidso
I am sick	sakútila
I am very sick	tiggã sakútila
are you sick?	nokútilá lah ?
he is not sick	to makútila
he is tired	istãstea

he is very tired	tiggä istástca
he is not tired	to istastca
are you not tired ?	to stanistcaki lah ?
where have you been ?	astákotci dislya?
what is your name ?	tatánisáta ?
I don't know	mátsikonishrá
I don't understand	tó nidistcl
do you understand	ni ditcaki lah ?
I have none	nítowá.

NOTES ON THE LANGUAGE.

It will be noted in the above vocabulary—

1. That the first, second, and third persons of the personal pronoun appear to be *sinna, ninna, iniila*; when used as possessives with a noun *si . . ., ni . . ., ma . . .*; and when governing a verb (*e.g.*, to smoke, *see* vocab.), *si . . ., ni . . . ., i. . . .* It appears, however, from the various verbs given in the vocabulary, that (if correctly obtained) there must be a great variation in the mode of forming the persons; and this, I expect, is due to their belonging to distinct paradigms.

2. The negative appears to be *to* prefixed to the verb. The Blackfeet Indians prefix *mat* to the verb, and follow it by *ats*. Ojibways prefix *kawin*, and end the verb with *si*. The Sioux simply use *shni* after the verb. Crees prefix *nämä*.

3. The interrogative particle appears to be *kilah*, or *lah* after the verb. Blackfeet express this by *kät* before the verb and *pa* after it. Ojibways by *nä*, Crees by *tci*, Sioux by *he*—all after the verb.

4. The numerals in this language are rather puzzling. There appears to be a double set. *Kositá* was given me as 5; yet 15 was *wiltaänmitañ*; and 50 took again the first form, *kositäté*. So with 16: *kostrani* is 6; *wistañmitañ*, 16; *kostrate*, 60. I notice also that the word for 6 seems to be an extension of the word for 3, and the word for 8 an extension of the word for 4. 10 seems to stand alone. The endings for the 'teens' being *mitañ*, which seems to have nothing to do with *kunisnän*. It seems curious also that the 'teen-ending' should be continued through the 'ties'; twenty-one would seem to be expressed in Sarcee as 10+11; but this is merely a surmise of mine, and if I knew more of the language I could probably explain these seeming irregularities. I may mention here, in connection with this, that the Ojibways count 1 to 5 with distinct words, then seem to begin 1, 2 again with the ending *waswi* from 6 to 10. Ojibways and Crees have almost the same words for the numbers 1 to 6, entirely different words for 7, 8, 9, and are nearly the same again for 10 and 20.

5. The plural of the noun appears to be *ika* or *a*. There does not appear to be any distinction made in the plural endings between animate and inanimate objects.

6. There does not appear to be any distinction made in the first person plural of the verb between 'we exclusive of the party addressed' and 'we inclusive.' In these two points (5 and 6) there is a decided divergence from languages of the Algonkin stock, and a leaning towards the Siouan.

7. *Ittra, ninna*, it seems, mean—the first, 'father,' or 'my father,' the second 'mother,' or 'my mother,' the possessive pronoun not being used in the first person for nouns of near relationship. This agrees with the Sioux.

8. The adjective follows the noun, the same as in the Sioux.

9. In the foregoing 260 words and sentences I do not recognise one word as similar to any word in any other Indian language with which I am familiar. But I have never before examined any of the 'Tinneh' or Athabascan stock. I might, perhaps, except *ninna, ni . . .* , the second person of the pronoun, which is analogous to *niye, ni . . .* of the Siouan dialects.

10. The sign of the past tense may be *te*, and of the future *ita* (see *smoke* in vocab.), but of this I cannot be sure.

11. The Sarcees seem to keep their lips parted while speaking, and the accent is generally on the *last* syllable of the word. The language has rather a clicking, 'slishing' sound.

12. In inflecting some of the verbs I have introduced the personal pronouns, but I imagine their presence is not necessary except for emphasis.

Notes by Mr. H. Hale on the foregoing Report.

Mr. Wilson's report on the Sarcees is specially valuable as being the only detailed account we possess of this interesting branch of the great Tinneh or Athabascan family. Some information concerning the tribe has been given incidentally by various writers, including Sir Alexander Mackenzie, Umfreville, and Petitot, but no particular description of the people has been heretofore published. It has been known merely that they spoke a dialect of the Tinneh language, and that they lived in close alliance with the Blackfoot tribes.

The Tinneh family, or stock, has attracted much attention from ethnologists, partly from the peculiar character of its members and partly from its wide diffusion, in which respect, as Mr. H. H. Bancroft has observed, it may be compared with the Aryan and Semitic families of the Old World. It occupies the whole northern portion of the American continent, from Hudson Bay to the Rocky Mountains, except the coasts, which belong to the Eskimo. Tinneh tribes also possess the interior of Alaska and British Columbia. Other scattered bands—Umpquas, Tlatskanais, and Kwalhioquas—are found in Oregon. The Hoopas and some smaller tribes live in Northern California. Thence, spreading eastward, Tinneh tribes, under various designations—Navahoes (or Navajos), Apaches, Lipanes, Pelones, Tontos, and others—are widely diffused over Arizona, New Mexico, Texas, and the northern provinces of the Mexican Republic.

The best account of the Northern Tinneh, east of the Rocky Mountains, is found in the introductory portion of the 'Dictionnaire de la langue Dèné-Dindjié' of the eminent missionary-philologist, the Abbé Petitot, who resided many years among them, and studied their languages, customs, and traditions with much care. In his list of the tribes belonging to this portion of the stock he makes a division styled mountaineers (*Montagnards*), possessing the country on both sides of the Rocky Mountains. The southernmost tribe of this division, on the east side of the mountains, is the Tsa-ttinnè, a name which he renders 'dwellers among the beavers.' The name is derived from *tsa*, beaver (which has various other dialectical forms, *tso, sa, za,* and *so*), and *tinnè* (otherwise *tenné, tena, atena, tunneh, dènè, danneh, dindjié,* &c.), the word for 'man' in the different dialects. M. Petitot describes the Tsa-ttinnè, or 'Beaver Indians,' as comprising two septs—a northern tribe, who hunt along the

Peace River, and a southern, who dwell about the head-waters of the
North Saskatchewan, towards the Rocky Mountains. The latter, he says,
are the *Sarcis*, who have separated themselves from the northern band.
The tribal name of Soténnä, which Mr. Wilson obtained from the Sarcees,
is evidently a dialectical variation of M. Petitot's Tsa-ttinnè.

It has been supposed that the separation of the Sarcees from their
Tinneh kindred, followed by their union with the Blackfeet, was the
result of dissensions among the Tinneh tribes. But the information
obtained by Mr. Wilson shows that this idea was not well founded. The
separation is now ascribed by the Sarcees to a superstitious panic, but
very probably resulted merely from the natural desire of their forefathers
to find a better country and climate. Their southward advance brought
them in contact with the Blackfeet, with whom they confederated, not
against their Tinneh kindred, as had been supposed, but against the Crees,
who have from time immemorial been the common enemies of the Tinneh
and Blackfoot tribes.

The legend of the deluge, which Mr. Wilson obtained, is given by
M. Petitot in a slightly different form, which on some accounts is worthy
of notice. In early times, we are told, there was a 'deluge of snow' in
September. This was changed to a flood of water by the act of 'the
mouse,' an important character in the mythology of some of the Tinneh
tribes, being regarded as 'the symbol or genius of death.' He pierced
the skin-bag in which 'the heat' was contained, and the snow was forth-
with melted. The flood quickly rose above the mountains and drowned
the whole human race except one old man, who had foreseen the
catastrophe and had vainly warned his neighbours. He had made for
himself a large canoe, in which he floated, gathering on it all the animals
he met. After a time he ordered several of these animals to dive and
seek for earth. These were the beaver, the otter, the musk-rat, and the
arctic duck. According to this version of the story, it was neither the
beaver nor the musk-rat that brought up the earth, but the duck. This
morsel of earth was extended by the breath of the old man, who blew
upon it until it became an immense island, on which he placed succes-
sively, during six days, all the animals, and finally disembarked himself.

This story is evidently made up from various sources. The skin-bag
of heat bitten through by the mouse seems to be a genuine Tinneh
invention. The diving of the animals, with the formation of the new
earth, is a well-known creation myth of the Algonkin and Iroquois tribes;
and the 'six days' are probably a late addition derived from the
missionary teachings. An inquirer among the Indian tribes is constantly
coming across such composite myths, which require careful study and
analysis.

Other observers agree with Mr. Wilson in regarding the Northern
Tinneh tribes as inferior in intelligence to the neighbouring Indians of
other stocks. This is doubtless a just view. The inferiority, however,
would seem to be not from any natural deficiency, but rather the result
of the very unfavourable conditions under which the former are con-
demned to live. Not much can be expected from bands of widely
scattered nomads, often famine-stricken, wandering over a barren region,
under inclement skies. In better surroundings their good natural
endowments become apparent. The Hoopas of California display much
intelligence and energy. Mr. Stephen Powers, in his account of the
'Tribes of California,' published by the American Bureau of Ethnology,

speaks of the Hoopas with much admiration, and styles them 'the Romans of Northern California'; he states that they had reduced most of the surrounding tribes to a condition of semi-vassalage. Mr. J. P. Dunn, an able and experienced writer, in his recent work, ' The Massacres of the Mountains,' describes the Navahoes as the most interesting of all the western tribes. They are a peaceful, pastoral, and agricultural people, remarkable for their industry and for their ingenuity in various manufactures. Their women weave excellent blankets, which, he says, ' have been the wonder and admiration of civilised people for many years. They are very thick, and so closely woven that a first-class one is practically water-tight, requiring five or six hours to be soaked through.' They make pottery, and ' have numerous silversmiths, who work cunningly in that metal.' Their women are well treated, are consulted in all bargains, and hold their own property independently. In 1884 the tribe numbered 17,000 souls, cultivated 15,000 acres of land, raised 220,000 bushels of maize and 21,000 bushels of wheat; they had 35,000 horses and 1,000,000 sheep. It has seemed proper to mention these facts as evidence that the Indians who inhabit so large a portion of British America, and whose descendants are probably destined to hold much of it permanently, belong to a stock which, under favouring circumstances, displays a good aptitude for civilisation.

M. Petitot, it should be observed, speaks of the Sarcee language as forming a connecting link between the languages of the northern and southern Tinneh tribes. Mr. Wilson's vocabulary, though taken under many disadvantages, will doubtless be found extensive enough to afford useful data to philologists in classifying the idioms of this important family.

The Committee ask for reappointment, with a renewal of the grant.

www.ingramcontent.com/pod-product-compliance
Lightning Source LLC
Chambersburg PA
CBHW021622290326
41931CB00047B/1423